Timeless Treasures
A Collection of Poems

Written by:
Gregory S. King

Edited, Formatted, Designed & Published

by

Wade Christian Publishing LLC

www.wadepublishers.com

info@wadepublishers.com

Timeless Treasures

A Collection of Poems

Written by Gregory S. King

ISBN: 979-8-9864810-7-4

Acknowledgements

To my wife, Cynthia King, children, family, friends, and a special thanks to Ms. Darlene Heaton, who has been instrumental in helping to inspire me to create this collection of poetry. To Mrs. Ruth Stepp and the late Jimmy L. Stepp who welcomed me into their home and adopted me as their son, thank you for your love and support; you have truly transformed my life. Also, to my church family, Fellowship of Praise; thank you for the continued prayers and support throughout the years. It is my prayer that the words in this collection will somehow encourage, inspire, bring hope, and maybe even laughter to many who are in various stages of life. In the times that we are living in……. WE ALL need to be encouraged!!!

Table of Contents

Life

Life is but a vapor that vanishes before the eye.
One moment we are born, and the next, we suddenly die.

We take for granted that the very next breath
Could be our last.
Do we realize the urgency and value of time which goes
By so fast?

Do we understand that life is a gift that should not be
Carelessly spent?
What do we do when that gift is gone, and we did not
Appreciate that which God has sent?

When the spirit of man is gone, the body is but a shell.
Yet, there is a story left behind that life can only tell.

Why do we take for granted the little things in life until
They are no longer there?
We cannot make up time that is not ours to
Spare?

Is it better to love and forgive than to take unrepentance
To the grave?
So, let us be reminded that only God has the power to
Heal, deliver, and save.

A New Song

Oh, sing a new song unto the Lord
All nations in the land.
Oh, sing a new song unto the Lord
For what He has done with His marvelous hand.

Oh, sing a new song unto the Lord
All people far and near.
Oh, sing a new song unto the Lord
With awe, reverence, and fear.

Rejoice in the Lord and bless His Holy name!
Rejoice, I say, and be not ashamed.

Oh, magnify the Lord with me!
For He has done marvelous things
Beyond what eyes can see.

My tongue shall make its boast in the Lord!
The humble shall hear and be glad thereof.
I will sing a song of praise to my God
Because He first showed me love.

Lord, I shall lift my voice and cry aloud
Unto thee.
Lord, your praise shall continually be in my mouth
Because you came and set me free.

Stop

Stop, and take a little time to meditate on the Word.
Stop, and ponder on that which you have heard.

Stop, and consider every move that you make.
Stop, and cherish each breath that you take.

Stop, and thank God for those little things He has done.
Stop, and thank God for giving His only begotten Son.

Stop, and rejoice when trials come your way.
Stop, and give God praise for seeing another day.

Stop, and show someone that God knows and He cares.
Stop, and tell someone that hell is real and eternal
Life can be theirs!

Stop, and appreciate the change of every season.
Stop, and realize that there is a time for all things
And everything has a season.

In Due Season

To everything under the heavens,
There is a purpose and a reason.
Wait on God, and you shall reap
In due season.

If we go before God then what we do
Shall not stand.
By Him, all things were made and
He does not need a helping hand.

Be careful about nothing, and always pray.
In all things, acknowledge God
And He will show you the way.

God knows what is best for us all
And He will not lead us wrong.
Commit your ways unto the Lord
And He will give you the strength to carry on.

We shall see the salvation of the Lord
If we only stand still.
The safest place in any storm is to remain in God's
Perfect and Holy will.

The Unknown god

Who is this god that doesn't respond at all?
Maybe he is deaf and cannot hear the call.

Or why do you speak to a god who doesn't
Know your name?
Maybe he's embarrassed, shy, or
Even somewhat ashamed.

Where is this god that you call on so earnestly
Morning, noon, and night?
Maybe it is because he is blind in both eyes
And cannot see how to fight.

Why has he not saved thee
And delivered thine life from hell?
Maybe it is because he did not have directions
And got lost for a spell.

Why doesn't he show himself and be put to the test?
Maybe it is because he is on vacation
And in need of dire rest.

Why doesn't this god answer swiftly by fire?
Maybe he is an imposter or just a servant for hire.

Is this god a magician pulling a rabbit out of the hat?
My, how shameful it is to serve a worthless god like that.

The Goat Mentality

I would have gone to church, but my job got in the way.
I could have made a better choice, but I didn't
Acknowledge God in any kind of way.

I know I need to change, but I refuse to repent,
Surrender, and obey.
I needed God's help, but I didn't know how
To pray.

It's time for Bible study, but there's a good show on
Tonight.
I should sing for God, but my voice just doesn't sound
Right.

I want God's blessings, but I want to do my own thing.
I know God is real, but I want Him on a string.

I want my family saved, but I'm not living right.
I can't wait on God, so I'll make it happen
With my own strength and might.

If I regard iniquity in my heart, the Lord will not hear.
Don't be like the goat who butts the head and has no fear.

How Far Is Too Far?

How much can one take before they go over the ledge?
When do we consider the dangers involved
Of pushing others too close to the edge?

How far will we go to drive home a point?
Oh, how the body feels much pain when the bone
Comes out of its joint.

Can we discern the heart of man when his soul
Needs time to heal?
Do we consider the weight on someone's shoulders
And have compassion for how they feel?

Do we know the pressures of enduring
Without rest down through the years?
We all need precious time alone, even to shed
Needful tears.

What happens if the body is not given
A chance to rest and unwind?
It, of course, shuts down, and we lose a peace of mind.

What happens to a tree that is not properly treated
Or handled with care?
It, of course, becomes unfruitful and not able to bare.

You Dish It, You Receive It

So easy it is for us to dish out; but how hard is it
For us to accept and receive the truth?
For respect of persons begins even in our youth.

God is not partial to showing favoritism nor respect.
Still, there are some that are cast aside, like they
Are worthy of neglect.

You esteem yourself so high, yet at the same time
You bring others down so low.
What is this secret
That you don't want others to know?

You push and shove continuously with a whip
Firm in hand.
How can anyone respond positively
And still be able to stand?

Things that should have been kept in secret
Have found themselves to be openly known.
How can people confide in you when
Trust cannot be shown?

Oh, how sharp it is when the Word cuts so deep.
Always know that when you dish something out,
The same you will also reap.

Great Is Thy Faithfulness

Great is thy faithfulness towards Me!
Look to those things from above and not
What your natural eyes can see.

For you have promised that nothing shall separate you
From My love within your heart.
Surely, you will be tried to see what can tear us apart.

What shall one give up that he
Might travel this journey all the way?
To be called and chosen, surely there is a
Very great price to pay.

You have been tried by the fire as silver and gold.
Even as the potter shapes the clay into a perfect
And excellent mold.

Arise, gird up thy loins, and like a trumpet, lift your voice.
Every man is persuaded by his mind and has been given a
Reasonable choice.

Cry loud with your voice and declare the Lord's Name!
Speak the Word only, and lives shall never be the same.

Busy Body

Diligently tending to other people's affairs.
Quick to be entangled and wrapped up in meaningless
Cares.

Too foolish to stand still, yet always itching to move.
Forever in the mix, trying to find something to prove.

A master at leading someone straight into the ditch.
Constantly conjuring things up like a nasty old witch.

Frequently changing colors like the chameleon on a tree.
Better yet, like a blind bat flying around,
Having eyes but cannot see.

Actively participating in all things; however,
Contributing at all to none.
Stretched out from here to yonder but getting nothing
Done.

Willfully causing mischief despite of what was said.
Hopelessly fluttering around like a chicken with no
Head.

Mamma

Superior and excellent in all of her ways!
We have only one whom we should cherish all of her days.

By her husband, she is praised, and her children call her
Blessed!
She is a woman of virtue known for the way she is
Dressed.

Compassionate, strong, and adorned
With grace.
Working diligently with her hands to keep all of her home
In place.

Nourishing and raising her children with discretion
And care.
All that we go through in life, Mamma is
Always there!

She is to be honored and respected.
Not to be taken for granted or neglected.

Each is unique and different in their own special way.
Let's thank God for our Mammas every single day!

I Worship

I worship You, Lord, just for who You are!
I worship You, Lord, the Rose of Sharon;
The bright and Morning Star!

I worship You, Lord, for being righteous and true.
I worship You, Lord, not for what You can do.

I worship You, Lord, for that which You have
Already done.
I worship You, Lord, for sending your
Only Begotten Son!

I worship You, Lord, for being the maker of all things.
I worship You, Lord, for being the King of all Kings!

I worship You, Lord, for enduring hardship and pain.
I worship You, Lord, for it is forever that You Reign!

Look To Jesus

For what shall it profit a man, if he shall gain the
Whole world and lose his own soul?
Where can we turn when the cares of the world
Has taken its toll?

Who can we lean on when no one else is there?
Who can we talk to when we have problems to share?

Where will we go when there's nowhere to hide?
How do I stay on a path that's not at all wide?

What can we do to be honest and real?
What can we take for the pain and hurt we feel?

How do we walk through this life from day to day?
Just look to Jesus because He is the way!

All That You Say

You are Alpha and Omega,
The beginning and the ending,
The first and the last!
You are the Creator of things to come, that are,
And of that in the past.

You are the true and living God, Almighty,
And Most High!
You gave Your only begotten Son; for our sins, He did
Die.

You know and see all that we do.
Many are called; however, You have chosen
Only a few.

You are all that You say, and besides You, there
Are no others.
You are closer than anyone, even sisters and brothers.

You are Omnipotent and just!
Only in You should we put
Our faith, hope, and trust.

Who Am I?

I did not come by in the darkness of night.
I came in the day to be seen as a light.

I did not use flattering words to entice.
I spoke from my heart and paid a great price!

I came not bragging or boasting, as in putting on a front.
I was humble and meek, gentle and blunt.

I came plain and ordinary, not dressed to appeal.
I came not deceiving; I was true and real.

I came to be received, but was persecuted and rejected.
I came to save those who are lost, and I died as expected.

I am wiser than a serpent, yet harmless as a dove.
I came to be a blessing, and to share my love.

The Battle Is The Lord's

Not by power, nor by might, but by the
Spirit of the Lord shall all things be done.
The battle is not yours, but with the Lord,
It has already been won!

If we live in the Spirit,
Then in the Spirit, we should also walk.
We should be doers of God's Word
And not as those who only talk.

Faith is evident in things we cannot see.
Submit yourselves, therefore, to God.
Resist the devil, and he shall flee.

You shall see the salvation of the Lord,
If you only stand still.
We shall reach that higher calling of God
If we stay in His will.

Lost Sheep

I was a misfit lost in an unknown land.
I was a stranger with a language
People did not understand.

I was as the waves tossed about
In the direction of the wind.
I was like a garment with colors that did not blend.

I was like a puppet whose master
Controlled him by a string.
I was like a bird that had no voice and could not sing.

I was like a crumb that was taken for granted.
I was like a seed that was waiting to be planted.

I was as a sheep that had gone astray.
I was surrounded by darkness
When light paved my way.

Compassion

A friendly smile goes very far.
It helps in mending any deep-felt scar.

Rejuvenating the soul from deep within,
Bringing about a change for
A new life to begin.

Even a gentle hug says a great deal.
It can let someone know that God cares
About how they feel.

On other occasions, a swift ear maybe required.
You must be prepared to labor even when tired.

Answering quickly is foolish and shows
A sign that you are weak.
However, hear and ponder the whole
Matter before you begin to speak.

Great is a man that makes himself humble.
But woe unto the man that causes
His brother to stumble.

Seek opportunities to show compassion
And love.
Not like the kind on earth, but like
The kind that is heavenly
From above!

(Eyes) Opened To The Truth

The Lord has brought us out of darkness; held captive in
Our hearts and minds.
We were bound by the sin that kept our eyes
Blind.

When Christ came into our lives, He allowed
Us to look back on the things that we
Used to do.
Our eyes were then opened to His Word, which is
Quick, powerful, and true!

We now understand that the Lord has brought
Us out of the muck and miry clay.
We are being transformed into new creations
Every single day.

Tight But Right

God's Word is like being whipped with a cord.
God's Word is sharper than any two-edged sword.

God's Word is more powerful than any magic that can
Be found.
God's Word comes as a thunderous and mighty
Sound.

God's Word purifies the heart of our temple.
God's Word is not hard, but clear and simple.

God's Word deals with the heart of man.
God's Word lets us know that He has a plan.

God's Word will correct and chastise.
God's Word helps us to be wise.

God's Word is the truth and the light!
God's Word maybe tight, but we must admit that
It is always right!

Precious

Your value is more than diamonds, rubies, or rare
Precious stone!
You are to be treated as a queen
And not as meat on a bone.

You are to be cherished and loved,
Reverenced and respected.
You are not to be taken for granted, neglected, or
Disrespected.

You are strong; however, to be handled with care.
You are virtuous indeed, wise, and fair.

You are compassionate and full of love.
You are peculiar and unique, like the stars above.

You are righteous, holy, and adorned with grace.
You are precious indeed, keeping all things in place.

A.W.O.L.

Present in the flesh yet absent in the mind.
The body is there, but the person we cannot find.

Wondering souls always seem
To get themselves lost.
Selfishly seeking validation
And not realizing the great price it will cost.

Open to dismiss oneself early
When war is raging at hand.
Closing the eyes to the truth and not having
A backbone to stand.

Quick to disappear and does not hang around.
Lost in space and cannot be found.

Loose at the lips and talks a big game.
Vanishes into thin air when the judge calls his name.

Tough as nails, he says, the best soldier to the end.
In the blink of an eye, he's gone with the wind.

God Ordains Marriages

Two are better than one.
By operating together, they are able
To get great work done.

The two shall be as one according to God's Holy Plan.
A wife is a helpmate for her husband
To add strength wherever she can.

A marriage is only honorable in
God's Righteous Sight.
Wait on the Lord, and be of good courage
Because He knows when the time is right.

When God does something, you will not
Have to wonder.
Because what God has joined together
Let not man put asunder.

A Word Of Prayer

May God bless your household day and night
Strengthening and guarding it with all His might

Keeping it fixed, stable, and rooted in His Holy Word
Allowing you to receive and do all that is heard

May the Word be the lamp for your feet
And the light that guides your way
Let it be the peace that passes all understanding
When there is nothing left to say

May truth reign supreme
And be the foundation on which you stand
Sufferings are but for a moment
Despite whatever darkness falls upon the land

May God hold and keep you in his loving arms
To shape you and mold you
To lead you and guide you
To protect you and shield you
From anything that harms

Amen

Worship

I humbly bow before Your throne.
I pay tribute and honor for the love You have shown.

I wait patiently in admiration kneeling before Your
Feet.
In the secret place of my closet is the place in which we
Meet.

To commune and fellowship is what
You desire.
It is an intimate relationship that will cause me
To go higher.

It is a time to share and express all of
What's on my heart.
It is a life lived in gratitude for what You have
Done from the start.
You are Almighty, and I worship you for being my
Creator.
You are self-existing, and there is no one
Greater.

You are the Wonderful Counselor, the Bright and
Morning Star!
Thou art the Anointed King, and I adore You just for
Who You are.

Be As Eagles

I will mount up with wings as eagles.
Soaring above all of my mountains.
I will fold my wings, swooping down to drink
From eternal fountains.

In the secret place of a rock on high
Will I dwell and make my nest?
I will seek and find food for my young
Before I take my rest.

I will cover them with my wings to protect
Them from any danger.
They will know my voice alone and will not
Hearken to that of a stranger.

I will discern my surroundings by using
My keen sight.
Though the wind blows, I will not be moved
While taking my daily flight.

With sharp talons, will I hold fast
And cling tightly to all good things.
I will embrace the true vine as I spread
My great wings.

Eagles are rare and peculiar birds.
As we are God's children,
Receiving and rightly applying all of His Holy Words.

Part-Time Lover

Who wants to be a part-time lover?
Who desires a fellowship that is kept undercover?

What woman waits faithfully
While we sleep with a complete stranger?
What wise person stays around to put their life
In total danger?

Who is the fool that desires to remain
In the cold and freeze?
What virtuous woman will lower herself to becoming
A tramp or sleaze?

A pimp doesn't care at all in the end.
He better have his money.
For he is smooth as silk and his words flow like honey.

Why be a fool and miss out for lustful pleasure?
The Lord commands to be first and not second by any
Measure.

Already Fixed

Be strong in the Lord and in the power of
His might.
Allow God's Word to lead and guide
You into that which is right.

Give up on your ways and come down off
Of your will.
When you are halting between two opinions,
Look to God and stand still.

The Lord cares, and He knows the heart of
Us all.
That is why there are blessings in store
For those that call.

The answer is nigh thee; even at thine door.
Just thank the Lord for all things when you
Kneel upon the floor.

Dedicated

We are dedicated to Christ, who lives inside.
We are dedicated to Christ and have
Nothing to hide.

We are dedicated to Christ because we believe
In His words.
We are dedicated to Christ, and are
Free from bondage like birds.

We are dedicated to Christ because He is strong
When we are weak.
We are dedicated to Christ, who is the Word
That we speak.

We are dedicated to Christ, for He is the rock
On which we stand.
We are dedicated to Christ, joined hand in hand.

We are dedicated to Christ, whose love is everlasting.
We are dedicated to Christ through prayers and fasting.

Wayward Israel

Awaken O' Israel thou that slumber and sleep.
How long shall you continue to work
And yet have nothing to reap?

You sow in bitterness and reap in despair.
Look now and see how you've gone nowhere.

How long shall you be taught like a child that
Is yet in school?
Or how long shall you refuse to grow
And be like that stubborn ole mule?

Who is it that examines the heart
And knows the thoughts of your mind?
Watch now and see that your ways will get you in a bind.

Despise not the chastening of the Lord; neither be thou
Bitter when you are corrected.
For if thou regard iniquity in thine heart, your prayers
Shall be rejected.

Turn now unto the Lord O' Israel; hear and
Obey.
For disobedience shall be disciplined, and the Lord shall
Repay.

That Ole Mule

The horse can be led to the trough, but who can make him
Eat?
What can make him budge when he is sitting down on his
Do-nothing seat?

Quite often, that ole mule can be a natural brute beast.
A stubborn ole mule he is, just to say the least.

Playing tug of war with that mule is like being in a brawl.
Who is it that can train a mule to answer every call?

Who wants a stubborn mule that causes so much
Pain?
Only that ole mule would do something silly like sit out in
The rain.

My, does he like to wonder about in his own ignorant
Way?
That ole mule; what is he good for but to make his
Master pray?

That ole mule does not even have the nerve to bow down
And let his master ride.
No bit and bridle, there's no hope at all to guide.

That poor ole mule cannot help how he is made.
So, think it not strange.
For it is in his nature to be what he is.
So how can he ever change?

My Deliverer

I will say of the Lord, He is my refuge
And fortress.
My God, in Him will I trust!
It is He that has created the heavens and the earth,
And formed man out of the dust.

He is my defense in the times of my distress.
He shall curse the wicked, and the righteous He shall
Bless!

He makes my ways to be straight,
And lights my path so that I may see
He will destroy the wicked and cause my enemies to flee.

Their evil devices shall slay them, and their wickedness
Shall come to naught.
I needed deliverance from my foes, and it was
The Lord that I sought.

With all my might, I cried unto the Lord,
Even with my last breath.
I feared no evil as I walked through the valley of the
Shadows of death.

The Thrill Is Gone!!!

This is what happens when the thrill is gone.
Our desire is not for fellowship but only to be left alone.

This is what happens when the thrill is gone.
Our minds grow carnal, and our hearts become as stone.

When the thrill is gone, we begin to argue and fuss.
When the thrill is gone, we blame others instead of
Finding fault in us.

When the thrill is gone, we become rebellious and bitter.
This is what happens when the thrill is gone; we make a
Mess of ourselves like a child needing a sitter.

When the thrill is gone, we walk out of love
And have no fear.
This is what happens when the thrill is gone; we have no
Joy and we lose our cheer.

What happens when the thrill is gone?
Misery loves company,
So, we find someone to tell.
This is what happens when the thrill is gone; we fail to
Repent and end up in hell.

I Am That I Am!

I have been fearfully yet wonderfully made!
I am created and fashioned of the most excellent grade!

Formed in the image of God am I!
I am on display to the world and watched by every eye.

I am of a rare and peculiar breed.
I am of a royal priesthood and born of a righteous seed.

I am joint-heirs to Christ with an inheritance in store!
I am seated in heavenly places enjoying treasures forever
More.

With loving kindness and tender mercies, I have been
Crowned.
I am more precious than any gem that is widely
Renowned.

Mercy and truth have not forsaken me,
and because of this, my favor is divine!
There is no one in this world that can have what's already
Mine!

Tongue Jury

Oh, how great destruction is made by the mouth
And the tongue.
For these are the members which causes
The whole body to be hung.

By this little thing, nations are divided, great and small.
It is also by this same thing that causes great
And mighty men to fall.

My, how the words come forth
Which spread smoothly like butter.
Yes, it is a puzzling thing, that tongue
Which has sweet and bitter words to utter.

Who can rule the tongue, that nasty old thing?
Imagine seeing that old tongue put a grown
Man in a sling.

Only the tongue can find an innocent man
Guilty as sin.
How deep and how wide is the pit that puts
The owner therein.

Oh, the tongue, that pink tornado
Which flaps all the time.
Sometimes good things come in small packages,
Yet they can also commit the greatest crime.

The Color Of Love

What is the color of love amongst the human race?
Does it even matter if love had a color on its face?

What is the color of love if life or death
Depended on its deed?
Is color that important to the one who's in dire need?

What is the color of love
If it had the power to set one free?
Does color really matter if the blind
Had sight to see?

What if love didn't have a color, but was like an image
That had no name?
What if skin had no color; would our love
Still remain the same?

What if love had no appearance; would we see beyond
Color and embrace the person within?
Should love really be determined
By the color of one's skin?

So, what is the color of love amongst
The human race indeed?
For it is but only to look beyond the barriers
And supply a desired need.

There Will Come A Time

There will come a time when mother nor father
Can save you from death.

There will come a time when you will be alone and
Have nowhere to go and no one to talk with.

There will come a time when it seems
Like giving up is the best thing to do.

There will come a time when you are
Lying in bed sick and praying that you were dead,
Or never had been born.

When times like these come, hold your head up
And smile; remember that God will
Never leave you when things get rough.

God will always by your side.
Since God created you, so shall He deliver
You in your worst of times.
Call on God when you are happy or sad.

Thank God for everything because He
(God Almighty) is the reason why
You live and breathe today.

Sweet Thing, Sweet Thing

Sweet thing, sweet thing, lend me your ear.
For my words drop as honey, so receive all that you hear.

Sweet thing, sweet thing, I have blinded thine eyes.
For it is by deception that you have accepted all my lies.

Sweet thing, sweet thing, I hold the key to your heart
Securely in my hand.
For I have taken your strength, and you have no
Backbone to stand.

Sweet thing, sweet thing, I will use what I have
To get what I need.
For I am in control, and you must follow my lead.

Sweet thing, sweet thing, Delilah is my name.
For you have been played like the fiddle,
And prostituted in my game.

Sweet thing, sweet thing, I have been sent by Jezebel,
The queen of all pride.
For she will stop at nothing to destroy and kill
The Lord's love and His bride.

Sweet thing, sweet thing, how foolish are you
To let down your guard.
For by my ways and actions, you disobey your Lord.

Empty Wagons

Empty wagons make a whole lot of noise.
Like the wheat and the tares, this walk will separate
The men from the boys.

Oh, how it hurts the ears when that old wagon goes past.
Apply a little pressure to a balloon, and its shape will not
Last.

Like an empty wagon good for nothing
Unless something is put therein.
Why put on a show for the devil when you're
Not at all any kin.

Yes, empty wagons have wheels, but they have no brakes.
God desires truth and reality, not imposters or fakes.

The Word says to stand, and not go around in circles,
Like the wagon with wheels.
For the way is straight, if one is led by the Word of God,
And not by what he feels.

Be not as the empty wagon sounding loud
And making much noise.
Let us grow to maturity in the Lord
And put away childish toys.

Foolish Galatians

O' foolish Galatians, who has bewitched thee?
Why go back to your vomit like the dog
When Christ has made you free?

Why should you be bound by the yoke
Of death and sin?
The devil doesn't care if you fall
So why be his friend?

How is it that you are so soon removed
From that which you have learned?
For every tree that bares no fruit is cast down
And utterly burned.

The blind cannot lead the blind
Or else they both fall into the ditch.
And he who disobeys instructions works craft
Like the witch.

The body cannot function at all except it have a head.
Know ye not that we are made alive in Christ
And no longer children of the living dead?

He who walks not in the council
Of the ungodly is known as a wise and blessed man.
But the foolish will do mischief and fall by his own plan.

Who's Loving Who?

Who's loving who; is the question I sometimes ponder?
Some say with their lips, "I love you Lord,"
But they travel here and yonder.

Who are they caressing, and what has their undivided
Attention?
What is it that has them bound or held captive
That they remain in detention?

Who's getting all the hugs and kisses morning, noon, and
Night?
What causes them to be missing in action, lost in space,
Or even disappearing out of sight?

Oh yes, it is the sound of sweet nothings
Being whispered in the ear.
It is the voice of another drawing them close and near.

He is the one who holds the key in the palm of his hand.
This is the stranger who makes them bow
In fear of his every command.

So, who is truly loving who?
Is love really the motive of why
They do what they do?

The Word Of God

The Word of God enlightens thine soul!
The Word of God shall make thee whole.

The Word of God brings us joy!
The Word of God gives us a hope that no man can
Destroy.

The Word of God keeps us content!
The Word of God is where our time should be spent.

The Word of God orders our ways.
The Word of God brightens our days!

The Word of God, we should delight ourselves.
The Word of God, keep it not on your shelves.

The Word of God gives us a peace of mind.
The Word of God is loving and kind.

The Word of God has picked us up.
The Word of God overflows our cup.

The Word of God is food to eat.
The Word of God, it tastes so sweet.

The Word of God will shape and mold!
The Word of God, it makes us bold.

In Times Like These

In times like these, we gather and come together.
In times like these, we all need one another.

But why be united only in times like these?
Will we be changed by the words we hear
Or will we continue doing as we please?

For in times like these, we reminisce
And remember moments shared in the past.
Now is the time to be determined and committed
In making those precious times last.

So let it not only be in times like these
We show appreciation and love.
Also, keep this in mind that it is God who knows
And sees all things from above.

Why is it mostly in times like these, that we express
Emotions and feelings of the heart?
Let this be the question we ask ourselves:
Was my love real at all and sincere from the start?

Wise Mule Stubborn Fool

I watched and observed as a mule and his master
Came riding along one day.
When suddenly, the mule came to a halt
For there was an angel of the Lord
Standing in the way.

The master could not see the angel
For he was blinded by the sin held deep inside.
So, he started to kick and beat the mule
Because he was filled with arrogance and pride.

The mule did not budge, nor did he move an inch.
For fear of the angel, he could not move
And neither did he flinch.

Yet, the master continued to torment the mule
With all his natural might.
Blinded by his sinful ways, the master
Could not perceive at all the angel before his sight.

Out of frustration, the master cried out Loudly with eyes
Bloody red.
Why don't you move you stubborn mule? Were the exact
Words that he said.

Shockingly the mule spoke and said, The Lord gave me
Wisdom to see the danger that lies ahead.
It is because of me, you foolish and stubborn man,
That you remain alive and not dead.

Doing Good Is Not Enough!!!

There was a man that did good all his life.
He had a loving family and cherished his wife.

The man went to church and paid all his dues.
He didn't smoke or cuss and stayed away from booze.
He had a great career and was well-respected in the city.
He was on the Board of Directors and Planning
Committee.

He also gave to charity and fed the community's poor.
He even gave the clothes off his back to some
Who knocked at the door.

Then a message was preached at church one day
That made him feel empty and scared inside.
He tried to smile the best he could,
But those feelings he just could not hide.

The message was about salvation and works
As far as he could tell.
As the message went on, his understanding was clear.
If a man does not accept Christ, he will surely go to hell.

The Fullness Of Time

When the fullness of time has come, and hearts
Are open to receive,
The eyes of our understanding shall be opened,
For then, we shall believe.

When the fullness of time has come,
And all shall be restored anew,
The tears in our eyes shall be wiped away,
And there will be no more trials for me and you.

When the fullness of time has come,
There will be joy forever more!
For eyes have not seen, neither have ears heard.
Neither have entered the hearts of men,
The things which God has in store.

When the fullness of time has come,
Our strength shall be renewed.
We shall be revived afresh as if
We had eaten natural food.

When the fullness of time has come,
We shall receive crowns as our reward.
Then we shall rejoice for eternity and be in the
Presence of the Lord!

Is It Worth It?

Shall we enter through the doors
Yet another day?
Shall we continue to transgress
And do things our own way?

Is it worth eternal life not to surrender all?
How long will we go astray
And not heed to His beckoning call?

How long will we continue to give
And make the same lame excuse?
Do our lives glorify God
Or is it only for our selfish use?

God sees all things, so tell me, do you know
Who's really the fool?
Who is it that has charge over our lives,
Is it God alone who has complete rule?

So, shall we go into this new day
With bitterness and strife?
For whom we serve now may determine
Where we spend eternal life.

My Defense

Fear not what man can do, nor the expressions
That are laid upon their faces.
For the wicked is for a little while; however, in the end,
It is their names God erases.

Be not afraid when you are delivered up
Into the hands of the judge.
Know that God has the final say
And His Word will not budge.

Though you are surrounded by serpents
And enclosed with briars,
It is the Lord that condemns every word
And frustrates the token of liars.

When mother and father forsake thee,
The Lord will take thee up.
He shall anoint thine head with oil,
And overflow thy cup!

If men fall all around you and cling to the dust,
Let the Lord be your strength and in Him put your trust.

Who Is It?

Who is it that listens and heeds to the cry?
Who is it that understands, in order
To live, you first must die?

Who is it that dares to spread the gospel
And is not truly ashamed?
Who is it that will be persecuted
For His Holy and Righteous Name?

Who is it that will save themselves
If you had to choose life or death?
Who is it that will be a voice for God
If it meant one last breath?

Who is it that will walk in love when
They know the lies are not true?
Who is it that will say, Father forgive them
For they know not what they do?

Have we at all ever suffered?
And indeed, have we endured any pain?
Have we walked for miles to hear the gospel
And eagerly stand waiting in the rain?

Can we even receive criticism
And accept our names being dragged through the mud?
Can we boldly and confidently
Drink from the cup of Christ's Holy blood?

United We Stand,
Together We Are Strong!!!

Let it be resolved that regardless of devastation and
Destruction,
We will not be dismayed by this world of corruption.

Let it be resolved that we will be joined hand in hand.
Even if it means taking our last breath.
For the grave has no victory, and Christ took
The bitter sting out of death.

Let it be resolved that despite tragedy;
The weight and heaviness of feeling empty and void,
Our faith is in God and shall not be destroyed!

Let it be resolved that our family is not limited
To any race, creed, color, or state.
Our trust is in God for He alone seals our fate.

Let it also be resolved that love conquers
And overcomes a whole multitude of sin.
So, instead of bitterness and vengeance, it was
Forgiveness we chose to extend.

Let it be further resolved that whatever weapon is
Formed against us shall not prosper, but indeed utterly
Fail.
So, it is by faith that you should know,
Because of Jesus Christ, the gates of hell shall not,
Will not and cannot ever prevail!

All Powerful

I make, form, and create all things that be!
That which is now, was created and brought forth
From that which eyes can't see.

I am He who spoke out of darkness
And called forth the marvelous light.
I am the One who separated the day from the night.

I alone created man in My image,
And formed him from dust.
Who else among men would you dare place your trust?

Who is the greatest than can measure My depth and
Height?
Who is it that can compare or come close to My strength
Or My might?

I am He who was, who is, and lives forever more.
I am the One who sets down kings
And uplifts those who are poor.

I have confounded that which is strong
And chosen what man has deemed weak.
I cause the wise men to be foolish when they open
Their mouths to speak.

I still the voices of thine enemies
And make their weapons to be of no effect.
Surely, I will overthrow kingdoms

And My children will I protect.

Steadfast And Be Strong

Be ye steadfast, unmovable, and in the work of the Lord,
Always abound.
Call upon the Lord while He is near; seek the Lord
While He may be found.

Let your delight be in the law of the Lord
And meditate therein day and night.
Be strong in the Lord and in the power of His might.

God did not give us a Spirit of fear, but of power, love,
And a sound mind.
Reach forth unto those things which are before
And forget those things which are behind.

Pressing towards the mark for the prize of the
Higher calling of God is a must.
For living by faith is the lifestyle of a person who is just.

Know that God is not an idol who sits by when you pray.
In fact, He knows and hears every single word that you
Say!

This Life

In this life, there are those who are sincere
In what they do.
In this life, there are those who tell only
Half of that which is true.

In this life, there are those who do things
To be seen of men.
In this life, there are those who will
Go to extreme measures so they might fit in.

In this life, there are those who tell everything they know.
In this life, there are those that look upon others
As if they were low.

In this life, there are those who never
Admit that they are wrong.
In this life, there are those who speak
Great and welling words with their tongue.

In this life, there are those who are
Humble and meek.
In this life, God is strong when we are weak.

In this life, we are sojourners, pilgrims passing
Throughout this land.
Heaven and earth shall pass away,
But in the end, only God's Word will be left to stand.

The Lamb Of God

As a precious lamb that was led to be slain.
Jesus took away our sins and bore all our pain.

As a lamb to be sacrificed that is Holy and pure.
Suffering many things in which He had to endure.

On the cross, amid sinners, is where He took his place.
He was lifted from the earth and drew all men
To look upon His face.

God was well-pleased with His Only Begotten Son.
Before His end, Jesus prayed, not my will Father,
But thine will be done!

When all was silent, His cry was heard throughout the
Land.
Jesus died and rose again with all power in His hands!

After putting all powers and principalities under His feet,
Jesus ascended to the right hand of the Father
And graciously took His seat!

God Is

Elohim, The Creator of the Heavens, the Earth, and the
Fullness thereof.
I worship and adore You, because You first showed me
Love!

El-Shaddai, God Almighty, through whom all Blessings
Flow!
You are the Supplier of all my needs, and a Giver of
Nourishment so that I may grow.

Adonai, My Lord, and My Master;
All-Knowing and All-Seeing!
You are Jehovah, the One and only Self-Existing Being!

Jehovah-Jireh, you are my Provider throughout the season.
You Are a God of Purpose, and to everything, there is a
Reason.
Jehovah-Shalom, You are my Peace in times of trouble
And storm.
You have clothed the lilies of the valley
And I know that You shall keep me warm.

Jehovah-Rohi, You are my Shepherd
And I shall not want for any good thing.
You are my protector and shield from whatever life may
Bring.

Highway to Hell

As I traveled down this highway I came to a place
Where I could see my death.
I stopped and realized that this was the place
Where I had taken my last breath.

I considered for a moment all the things
That I had done in the past.
I realized that at a young age my life had ended too fast.

I turned aside and saw all the things
That I had ever done wrong.
I realized that my life on earth was not very long.

I turned again and saw a huge gate that was opened
Very wide.
I saw all the demons waiting for me as I came and
Peeked inside.
I saw all the times I disobeyed what my parents had
To say.
I realized that I had ignored all the warning signs
Posted along the way.

In this place, there was crying, screaming, and a very
Nasty smell.
I realized at that moment that this was the highway that
Took me straight to hell.

Mouth All Mighty

What is faster than a speeding bullet I wonder?
What is extremely small yet able to cause chaos and
Plunder?

What can leap tall buildings in a single bound?
What can make the whole world turn upside down?

What is more powerful than a locomotive or cargo train?
What can cause wise men to turn backward and go
Insane?

What is mightier than the wind which cannot stand still?
What can wound, mend, heal, and kill?

What is smoother than silk and spreads better than
Butter?
What can cause one to rise like the sun
And make the rich man fall flat in the gutter?

What can create something out of nothing
And boast of great things which are to come?
What is it, you ask? Why, it is the mouth that causes
The man to look simple, foolish and dumb.

Time Ran Out

Tick, tick, tick, goes the hand on the clock.
At the instance of death, some may faint, while others
Go into shock.

Immediately, they see what could have been their very
Own end.
Yet, they continue to indulge in and uphold a sinful
Lifestyle they choose to defend.

Could I really be next? They ask with fear and
Trembling in the voice.
The reality is, that death has no time frame on when we
Make our choice.

What if time ran out before repenting to God above?
What if time ran out before reconciling with those we
Love?

What if time ran out before we said goodbye?
What if time ran out right when you told that lie?

What if time expired during your praise and shout?
Will you be the one who accepts the Lord before your time
Runs out?

Sanctified Saint

I've been hoodwinked, bamboozled by that sanctified
Saint.
I've been sliced and diced by that lying ole saint.

I was deceived by the one who wasn't His from the start.
I've been given a false drawing of worthless fake art.

I've been handed with confidence a crisp counterfeit bill.
I was slipped a mickey and given a poisoned pill.

I've been duped and conned by that saint who claims
They're His.
I was flattened to the core like a soda with no fizz.

That sanctified saint blended in so well, like the
Chameleon on a tree.
That saint drove me into the ditch, like the blind man
Who couldn't see.

I was shipwrecked and abandoned, with no boat
Plainly in sight.
That saint came through like the wind or a thief
In the dark of night.

I was caught unaware like a fish on a hook.
So, beware of those who say they're a sanctified saint;
Because it may turn out to be that they're a wretched ole
Crook.

Web Of Lies And Deceit

Oh, how the web is tangled when we practice lies and
Plan to deceive.
They are the fools, we say, when we expect them to
Believe.

The words flow with ease, with no hesitation at all.
No remorse, no conviction, but with audacity and gall.

When practice is perfected, then it becomes a profession.
The heart is not condemned and there is no confession.

Skillfully waiting for the right time to spring the trap,
Waiting for your victim to fly faithfully in the lap.

What an intricate design is the web by its master.
The prey is unaware of the looming disaster.

One lie, two lies, three lies, four.
A never-ending cycle and so much more.

Deceiving and being deceived by the choices we make.
Not being able to distinguish what's real and what's
Fake.

But what happens when the master is caught
In the web made of deceit and lies?
That same web finds him trapped, then he suffers and
Dies.

About the Author

Gregory S. King is married to Cynthia D. King. They have three daughters (Arielle King, Armani King, & Olivia Rivera), an adopted stepdaughter (Tanza Hoheb), four grandchildren, and one great-grandchild. He is a faithful member of Fellowship of Praise Church in Santee, SC, and has served in various capacities: Deacon, Youth Sunday School teacher, sound technician, and computer repair person.

Mr. King lives in Santee, SC, and is a Holly Hill Roberts High School graduate. He has a certificate in leadership through the L.O.U.D. Leadership Program sponsored by Senator John W. Matthews. Mr. King has earned a Bachelor of Science degree in Organizational Management and a Master of Business Administration degree from Claflin University. He has also earned a Master of Science degree in Cybersecurity from Webster University. In 2010, Mr. King won the election for councilmember in the Town of Santee, SC, where he currently serves. His motto is – "Together We Can Do Great Things!"